Copyright © 2013 Aaron R. Lema—All rights reserved.

All rights reserved; that means do not reproduce, copy, translate, or transmit any part of my book in any way, electronically, photographically, mechanically, or even manually, without first obtaining my written permission to do so—which you do not currently have. An exception is made for news outlets, in the case of brief quotations embodied in critical—or not so critical—news articles and news reviews. Also, downloading it from the Internet, without paying for it, is the same as stealing it; so don't do that either.

Note: Some material in this book previously appeared in *Humanatapilism: An economic model to improve humanity and unscrew free market capitalism* by Aaron R. Lema, copyright © 2012 Aaron R. Lema. That book was never made available to the public, as it was deemed too boring for public consumption; it was shared only with a few people in the media, a few people in the publishing industry, and a few professors in the field of economics. Besides, that title, *Humanatapilism: An economic model to improve humanity and unscrew free market capitalism*—sucked something awful.

Attention: This book contains the opinions, ideas, and humor of its author—which some may find utterly offensive, totally insensitive, or downright stupid. Its sole intent is to provide helpful, hopefully useful, information on the subject matter being covered—*Humanatapilism: An economic model to unscrew humanity and improve free-market capitalism*. This book is made available to you with the understanding that I, author Aaron R. Lema, am not engaging in rendering professional services to you in any way. If you require professional financial services or need a financial professional's advice, you must consult with a competent financial professional.

Don't blame me: I have enough B.S. in my own life to deal with; I do not need your B.S. too. I accept no responsibility for your actions, nor do I assume any liability for your actions. If you experience a loss, personally or in your business, which is incurred as a consequence, directly or even indirectly, from the use or implementation of the economic model of Humanatapilism into your personal life or business, then that loss is entirely on you.

Thank you for reading this section: Believe it or not this section of the book took two hours to write. Making something as boring as copyright information and disclosures interesting is not as easy as it may seem; those are some boring topics. So if you have read this far, I am assuming that they were interesting enough to keep your attention—or you have an obsessive-compulsive personality that makes you read every section of a book. Either way, I thank you for taking the time to read this section, and for purchasing my book.

Contents

Introduction to Hu-MAN-ah-TAP-il-ism

Economics: "I spent a few bucks, top dollar, who gives a shit?"

The Big Three—and Me: Influential Economic Thinkers

    Karl Marx: Profit's Exploitation!
    John Maynard Keynes: Government Should Help
    Adam Smith: It's the Invisible Hand
    And Me—Aaron R. Lema: The World Could Suck Less!

A New Ism: "What we've got here is . . . failure to communicate"

The Economic Model (Ism): "One Piece at a Time"

    Humanatapilism
    Objective
    The Economic Model's Premises
    Now, One Piece at a Time

The Author, the Baker, and the News Anchor: Humanatapilism at Work

    The Author—Aaron R. Lema
    The Baker—Marvin
    The News Anchor—William O'Malley

People in a Humanatapilism Economy: Government's Role, How to Participate, How Not to Participate

    Humanatapilism Is a Form of Free-Market Capitalism
    How to Participate
    How Not to Participate

Charitable Organizations: The Catalyst of the Humanatapilism Economy

    The Purpose of Charitable Organizations
    Choosing a Charitable Organization
    Look Before You Leap

Don't Even Think About It! When to Exclude Businesses from Humanatapilism

    Temporarily Excluded from Humanatapilism
    Permanently Excluded from Humanatapilism

Final Thoughts

My Goal: Raise $1,000,000 For Charity

Introduction to Hu-MAN-ah-TAP-il-ism

Humanatapilism: An economic model. And what is an economic model? It is a theoretical construct; it represents economic processes by a set of variables and a set of logical and/or quantitative mumbo-jumbo type relationships with technical jargon and/or crazy words and blah blah blah blah blah....

Please, allow me to start over.

Introduction II

"How do you eat an entire elephant?" "One bite at a time."

And what does eating an entire elephant one bite at a time have to do with an economic model? Well, I believe that question and its answer represent a simple approach to solving a large problem; it's an approach I feel can be used to explain humanatapilism, my economic model—so here goes.

"How do you explain humanatapilism?" "One piece at a time."

"One piece at a time" will allow me to explain the economic model of humanatapilism in its *simplest terms*; it will also help keep you, the reader, from getting bored. Or to quote my mom, "Aaron, reading a book on economics would be as boring to me as reading the full-page, fine-print, legal disclosures for male erection dysfunction medications in a sports magazine." That was tough to hear from my mom, but her point was well made: Keep it simple, short, and interesting to read. At least, I hope that was her point.

So to keep it simple, short, and interesting for you, the reader, I will do the following. First I will not bloviate—that means I won't use technical jargon or overly wordy explanations. Second, I will keep the book under 30 pages—short and to the point. Third, I will inject humor—with absolutely no guaranties as to its funniness.

Thank you for purchasing my book, *Humanatapilism: Unscrew Humanity & Improve Capitalism—Part Deux*; by doing so you have put me one step closer to achieving my goal of raising $1,000,000 for charity.

Economics

"I spent a few bucks, top dollar, who gives a shit?"
—Nicky Santoro, from the movie *Casino*

Believe it or not Nicky Santoro's statement is an example of economics at work. Let me explain. Nicky Santoro knew the FBI was watching him and that they were spending a lot of money to do it, so he spent a few bucks on counter-surveillance equipment to be able to watch the FBI. That's economics at work. And here's why. So he spent a few bucks; his illegal mob activities generated lots of bucks—douchebag bucks—and anyone who's completed elementary school knows that lots of bucks is more than a few bucks. And whenever you spend a few bucks to make a lot of bucks, or to protect a lot of bucks in Nicky Santoro's case, you're making a good economic decision. A bad economic decision is spending a lot of bucks to make a few bucks—because a lot is more than a few. And that's where the "who gives a shit?" portion of his statement comes into play: He may have made a bad economic decision, by spending a lot of bucks to protect a few douchebag bucks. After all, he was a drugged out sociopathic gangster with a bad case of the peek-a-boos—his decision-making process may have been a little fuzzy.

Now you're not a drugged out sociopath with a bad case of the peek-a-boos—at least I am assuming you're not—and you might not have seen the movie *Casino*, so my movie reference may have made little sense to you. So why should you care about economics? I'll tell you why: Because economics affects every aspect of your life—yes, *every* aspect. And you'd better know a little about it, because claiming ignorance of economics is just like claiming ignorance of the law, neither system will grant you a reprieve when you violate—knowingly or unknowingly—one of its core principles. So knowing some economic basics is a must. And possessing a little common sense doesn't hurt, either. For the sake of moving forward I'll trust that you possess common sense—please don't make me regret it.

Basically, economics is the study and analysis of the ways in which societies produce and distribute goods and services. Okay, that explanation is pretentious; let me give you two from everyday life. Every time you buy a car, and every time the car dealer sells you a car, you're both dealing in economics. And every time you locate a lawyer to represent your uncle, Big Sal, for doing something to someone, over who knows what, and that lawyer agrees to represent him by taking your money, you're dealing in economics. It's that simple—well it's almost that simple. We as a society work within an economic model, a kind of an overall rule book for our economic behaviors if you will, and that's where it gets a little complicated.

Remember: Economics is the study and analysis of the ways in which societies produce and distribute goods and services. So before I move on, I want to introduce you to three of the most influential economic thinkers and their economic models. Now why would I do that to you? Because these three men have affected economies around the world, and if you live in an economy, which you do, you'd better get acquainted with these three men, because in one way or another they have affected your personal economy, and that of your nation—that's why.

The Big Three—and Me

Influential Economic Thinkers

"Generally, the theories we believe we call facts, and the facts we disbelieve we call theories." That profound statement was from Felix S. Cohen, an American lawyer and philosopher, and his statement most certainly applies to economics. Over the centuries, great thinkers, philosophers, scholars, a few dictators, and megalomaniacs all developed economic theories, or models, in the hopes of explaining society's economic behaviors. Some of their economic theories, or models, benefited societies, and some had very detrimental effects on societies. For simplicity's sake, and to keep from boring you to death, I will introduce you to the big three—and most influential—economic thinkers: Karl Marx, John Maynard Keynes, and Adam Smith.

Attention Die-hard or radicalized Marxists, Keynesians, and Smithians: This is only a synopsis of their economic theories—so don't get all butt hurt if I leave out something you feel passionate or fanatical about.

Karl Marx: Profit's Exploitation!

Karl Marx was a German political scientist and economist who lived from 1818 to 1883. Marx was a true cynic when it came to the capitalist system: He believed that a capitalist's profit came solely from exploiting labor. Marx's economic theory was that the capitalist system's exploitation of labor would lead to economic instability, and that economic instability would eventually lead to an economic collapse; therefore, he could not abide the notion of a profit-oriented economic system. Marx also predicted that capitalism would ultimately fail and that economies around the globe would quickly move toward communism, in which "labor" (that is, the state) would own the means of producing and distributing goods and services, thus eliminating the need to "exploit labor" for profit. Clearly, Marx's economic theory had tremendous impact on many economies and societies around the globe; just take a look at the economic policies of the former USSR, Cuba, and Venezuela.

In reality, however, two undisputable facts undermine Marx's theory. First, the wages of "laborers" (or workers) have actually risen over time. This fact alone destroys Marx's theory that labor is exploited in the name of profit in a capitalist economy: If the workers' incomes are rising, they are clearly sharing in the profits being earned. And finally, communist (centrally planned) economies, have proven to be far less efficient at distributing goods and services—that is, at creating the greatest good for the greatest number of people in a society—than capitalist economies.

While I am in no way a Karl Marx fan, and Marx's theories have been discredited, they are worth looking into, because knowledge is power. Two of Marx's books, *Capital*—volume 1, and *The Communist Manifesto* cowriten with Frederick Hegel, are boring and full of idealistic hoopla, but they are worth a read—they also cure insomnia. Okay, I have no medical proof that Marx's books cure insomnia, all I know is ten to eleven pages into one of Marx's books and I fall so deep into REM sleep that drool pours from my mouth like a waterfall.

John Maynard Keynes: Government Should Help.

John Maynard Keynes was a British economist who lived from 1883 to 1946. Keynes' approach to economics favors the government's power to tax, borrow, and spend to keep the economy stable and growing. And Keynes primary economic theory is that there is only one way out of an economic recession or depression, and that's for the government to start spending money. Keynes' reasoning was that government spending put money back into the pockets of the private sector; and when the private sector had money in their pockets, their demand for goods and services would also rise; and when the demand for goods and services would rise—the economic recessions or depressions would end. Also, Keynes was developing his economic theories during the Great Depression, a time when millions of people lost their life savings—and jobs, and the collapse of economic activity around the globe was thought to be the end of the capitalist system. So Keynes needs to be cut a little slack: The hardship he saw people endure, along with the attacks on capitalism he witnessed, had to have had an influence on his economic theories—how could it not have?

However well-intentioned Keynes may have been, his economic theories proved to be wrong and very short sighted. My analysis is based on our current economic climate—or should I say our current political climate—with its "government should spend, spend, and spend our way back into economic prosperity" mentality, and on the fact that our national debt is $16,000,000,000,000 and rising as a result of all the government spending—with absolutely no real economic prosperity to show for it. Therein lies the rub: Even if our government spends itself into bankruptcy—*which it is currently doing*—and our economy still does not rebound from its recession, believers in Keynes' economic theory can always state, "It could've worked—if our government would have just spent more money."

Adam Smith: It's the Invisible Hand.

Adam Smith was a Scottish philosopher who lived from 1723 to 1790. Smith's primary economic theory was that a *laissez-faire*—or "allow to do"—attitude by the government toward the marketplace would allow the "invisible hand" to govern everyone's economic activities. Essentially, Smith believed that, collectively, the individuals in a society, each of them acting in their own self-interest (earning a profit), would manage to produce and purchase the goods and services that they as a society would need. And all of this would be accomplished without the king—or the government—telling them when, where, why, and how they should do it. Basically, the "invisible hand" is the free-market at work in a society.

Adam Smith is also known as the founder of modern day economics. Smith's theory of the "invisible hand" has given many philosophers, scholars, economists—and me—lots to think about and to build upon.

And Me—Aaron R. Lema: The World Could Suck Less!

My economic theory is this: The world could suck less. Humanatapilism was developed with that simple theory as its core principle—because the world could suck less.

A New Ism

"What we've got here is . . . failure to communicate"
—The Captain, from the movie *Cool Hand Luke*

People may be either emotional or rational about economic issues. Unfortunately, those people who are primarily emotional about economic issues view the people who are primarily rational about economic issues as narrow minded and uncaring. Similarly, those people who are primarily rational about economic issues view the people who are primarily emotional about economic issues as narrow minded and whiney. So, what we have here is . . . failure to communicate. This failure to communicate has to end; people must adjust their primary view of economic issues—*so they can unscrew humanity*.

A new Ism is needed, an Ism that is both emotional and rational. So what we'll have here is . . . effective communication when it comes to economic issues. The new Ism I am proposing is *humanatapilism*, a modified version of our current economic system of free-market capitalism. The modifications I am suggesting are in one sense immense, but in another sense very small. For example, I do not suggest that we fundamentally change our current economic system. Instead, I reason that what we need to do is modify our current economic system to be both emotional and rational so we can communicate effectively when it comes to economic issues. The effective communication of economic issues *will improve capitalism*.

The very idea that we modify our current economic system to be both emotional and rational may of course, seem immense. But it is not impossible. This new Ism is a modified version of something people are already familiar with; it's fundamentally free-market capitalism. In other words, humanatapilism is in no way a radical transformation of our current economic system. In fact, I believe it is a natural fit because people are both emotional and rational about economic issues. This brings us to the next problem.

The suggestion that people adjust their primary view of economic issues is controversial. But it is not that hard to do—people are both emotional and rational. All the emotional people need to remember is that a rational person's black-and-white view of economic issues is helpful; it provides clarity and gives us a sense of direction. All the rational people need to remember is that an emotional person's non black-and-white view of economic issues is helpful; it reminds all of us that our economic issues are made up entirely of people. This should give every one of us a sense of direction.

A simple way to adjust our primary view of economic issues is to adopt a more realistic economic model, Ism, as a guide. The economic model of humanatapilism outlined in this book is both emotional and rational. This new approach can adjust our primary view of economic issues, and this will *unscrew humanity* and *improve capitalism*.

I believe the switch to an economic model that is both emotional and rational will be easy, and I believe after reading this book you will find it easy too.

The Economic Model (Ism)
"One Piece at a Time"

Humanatapilism

The belief that improving the quality of life of your fellow human beings *through* free market capitalism is the right way to succeed and improve one's own quality of life.

Objective

Unscrew humanity and *improve free-market capitalism.*

The Economic Model's Premises

Since people are both emotional and rational about economic issues, the most effective economic model ought to incorporate this dual emotional/rational approach.

Humanatapilism is the only economic model with the dual emotional/rational approach required to *unscrew humanity* and *improve free-market capitalism.*

Humanatapilism: Humanity + Capitalism (Emotional + Rational).

> *Humanity (Emotional):* For the purpose of the model, humanity is defined thus:
>
>> If each man or woman could understand that every other human life is as full of sorrows, or joys, or base temptations, of heartaches and remorse as his own, how much kinder, how much gentler they would be.
>> —William Allan White
>
> *Capitalism (Rational):* For the purpose of the model capitalism is defined thus:
>
>> What kind of society isn't structured on greed? The problem of social organization is how to set up an arrangement under which greed will do the least harm; capitalism is that kind of system.
>> —Milton Friedman

Humanatapilism: A form of free-market capitalism.

> *Humanatapilism:* The belief that improving the quality of life of your fellow human beings *through* free market capitalism is the right way to succeed and improve one's own quality of life.
>
> *Humanatapilist:* Any person or business *willingly* and *honestly* participating in an economy based on humanatapilism.
>
> *Humanatapilizing:* Profiting from humanatapilism in a *fraudulent* manner, or, *forcefully* imposing humanatapilism onto a person or business through political actions or social pressures.

---

1   Note: My use of "squared" in this book refers to the fourth dimension of profit, which I'll explain later.

The humanatapilism formula:[1]

$$P\text{ squared} = P(R - T = N) + D = Q$$

The humanatapilism formula represents a four-dimensional hyperspace, which has a singularity at its origin, in a three-dimensional reality. P is the singularity, the starting point, and the variables R, T, N, D and Q represent things P has a direct effect upon. In the humanatapilism formula, P is both a physical quantity and a mathematical constant.

I would like to take a moment to thank John Forbes Nash, Jr. for his personal equation $B\text{ squared} + RTF = 0$. John Forbes Nash Jr. received a Nobel Prize in economics, and his life story was the basis for the motion picture, *A Beautiful Mind:*

> Thank you, John Forbes Nash, Jr. Your personal equation and brilliant explanation of it inspired me, even though I have no idea what it means.

Now, One Piece at a Time

"Aaron, I hope you can explain that formula using simpler language, because if you can't, people will think you're crazy, or worse, they'll think you're full of shit." I would like to thank my mom, Claire Lema, for her inspiring words of wisdom.

> Thanks, Mom. I will heed your advice; I will explain the formula using simpler language, and I will do it *one piece at a time*.

The formula's variables—the basic pieces: P = Profit, R = Revenue, T =Total expenses, N = Net profits, D = Donation, and Q = Quality of life.

More specifically:

P = Profit—the compensation a business earns when it successfully increases the value of its resources into more highly valued products or services.

R = Revenue—the total dollar amount a business generates.

T = Total expenses—the total dollar amount a business spends to generate revenue.

N = Net profit—the positive dollar amount a business earns when it successfully generates more revenue than total expenses.

D = Donation—the resources (dollars, products, services, or expertise) a company provides to charitable organizations to improve the quality of life of our fellow human beings.

Q = Quality of life—the positive effect a humanatapilist business has on people when its donations do not have a negative impact on profit.

Profit: The singularity (the point of origin). You can't have one (donation) without the other (profit). Profit is needed to continually generate revenue, total expenses, net profit, donation, and quality of life, while the generation of revenue, total expenses and net profit is needed to continually generate profit.

One exists only because of the other: Revenue, total expenses, net profit, donation and quality of life would not exist without *the successful earning of profit*.

The three-dimensional reality. The three-dimensional reality in the formula is represented by the variables R, T and N, shown in the formula as "$(R - T = N)$."

$(R - T = N)$, or *Revenue minus Total expenses equals Net profit,* is the three-dimensional reality in which a successful business operates in a free-market capitalist economy.

The success-failure structure of a free-market capitalist economy is clear; those businesses generating more revenue than total expenses will earn a net profit equaling success, and those businesses generating less revenue than total expenses will earn losses equaling failure.

The four-dimensional hyperspace—*theoretical space* **having more than three dimensions.** The four-dimensional hyperspace in the formula is represented by the variables R, T, N and D.

$(R - T = N) + D$, or *(Revenue – Total expenses = Net profit) + Donation,* represents the four-dimensional space a successful business *seeks* to occupy.

The successful-only structure of the four-dimensional space is clear: Only a successful business generating more revenue than total expenses, thus earning a net profit, may *seek* to occupy the four-dimensional space by adding donation.

P squared. In the formula, P squared $= P (R - T = N) + D = Q$, or *Profit (Revenue – Total expenses = Net profit) + Donation = Quality of life,* represents the successful addition of donation.

The success-failure structure of a humanatapilism economy is clear; a successful business capable of adding donation without having a negative impact on revenue, total expenses and net profit will experience success in a humanatapilism economy, while a successful business experiencing negative impacts to revenue, total expenses and net profit because of their donation will experience failure in a humanatapilism economy.

Profit: a physical quantity and a mathematical constant.

Profit as a physical quantity—the numbers used to express Revenue, Total expenses, Net profit and Donation. In the formula $(R - T = N) + D$, if R is $200,000, T is $125,000, N is $75,000, and D is $12,500, the example then looks like this:

($200,000 – $125,000 = $75,000) + $12,500

Simply stated, a successful business generating Revenue of $200,000 with Total expenses of only $125,000 will earn a Net profit of $75,000; it will then seek to add a Donation of $12,500.

Profit as a mathematical constant—the percentage used to compute Donation. In the formula $(R - T = N) + D$, if R is $200,000, T is $125,000, N is $75,000, and D is 10% of $125,000, the example then looks like this:

($200,000 – $125,000 = $75,000) + (10% of $125,000)

Simply stated, a successful business generating Revenue of $200,000 with Total expenses of only $125,000 will earn a Net profit of $75,000; it will then seek to add a Donation of 10% of Total expenses to charity.

Humanatapilism *recommends* your donation be no less than 2.5% of your revenue, total expenses or net profit, with a maximum donation of 10% of your revenue, total expenses or net profit. Anything less than 2.5%, I believe, would be too little a contribution to charity, while anything over 10% may negatively impact your business profit. *Donate what you are successfully able to.*

Where'd Q go? Q, or *Quality of life*, cannot be quantified—it's an emotional, physical and spiritual state of well-being. And that poses a serious problem for economists. The world of economics, it would seem, will only work if something can be quantified. So, how does one quantify quality of life? Make it a variable of profit. As a variable of profit, quality of life can now be quantified. Q, or *Quality of life*, as a variable of profit, is expressed as D, or *Donation*.

Donation—the resources (dollars, products, services, or expertise) a company provides to charitable organizations to improve the quality of life of our fellow human beings. Here are three ways to calculate D:

D = **Revenue**—the total dollar amount a business generates. D can be a percentage of revenue ($D = 10\%$ *of R*) or it can be a set amount taken from revenue ($D = \$12,500$).

D = **Total expenses**—the total amount a business spends to generate revenue. D can be a percentage of total expenses ($D = 10\%$ *of your products, services or expertise*) or it can be a set amount taken out of total expenses ($D = 10$ *of your product, 10 hours of your service, or 10 hours of your expertise*).

D = **Net profit**—the positive amount a business earns when it successfully generates more revenue than total expenses. D can be a percentage of net profit ($D = 10\%$ *of N*) or it can be a set amount taken from net profit ($D = \$12,500$).

So, what exactly is Q, or Quality of life? The best way of explaining the variable Q or Quality of life is to break it down into its emotional and rational aspects. The emotional and rational aspects of Q, or Quality of life, are defined in humanatapilism thus:

Emotional:

> How selfish soever man may be supposed, there are evidently some principles in his nature, which interest him in the fortune of others, and render their happiness necessary to him though he derives nothing from it, except the pleasure of seeing it.
> —Adam Smith

One of the best reasons people donate to a charitable organization is the heightened sense of physical, emotional, and spiritual well-being they experience when they help to improve upon the physical, emotional, and spiritual sense of well-being of someone less fortunate. Humanatapilist donation in its purest form is always done with this intention.

However, we must be willing to accept the fact that our physical, emotional, and spiritual sense of well-being, and the physical, emotional, and spiritual sense of well-being of some one less fortunate, is not the only aspect to consider: *Quality of life has a price.*

Rational:

> There's no such thing as a free lunch.
> —Milton Friedman

Humanatapilism instructs businesses to be rational, un-humanly rational, some might say. I trust by now you have some sense of what it is I mean by that. The emotional and rational approach taken by humanatapilism toward economic issues allows for businesses to look out for their profits, and it allows for businesses to direct some—a *set amount* or a *percentage*—of their profits into a donation for charitable organizations.

Quality of life has a price, and that price is donation. To find the price of quality of life, businesses must calculate how much they can donate to a charitable organization without negatively impacting their profits, *the businesses' own quality of life*. For example, say a new humanatapilist business wants to donate $10,000 to a charitable organization, but it does not want to exceed 10% of its revenue to do it. We can also say, in the case of this example, that the business believes the donation will not have a negative impact on its revenue, total expenses, or net profit. The business comes to the end of its physical year and it has earned only $90,000 in revenue. The business then calculates its donation of $10,000 to be 11.1% of its revenue, which it decides is way too much to donate, as that amount may have a negative impact on its revenue, total expenses, and net profit for the following year. The business then decides to make a donation of $9,000, or 10% of its revenue, to the charitable organization to improve upon the quality of life of our fellow human beings. This means the business implicitly values Quality of life at $9,000, or 10% of its revenue.

Now, let's say a business that manufactures children's shoes wants to make a donation of 7,500 pairs of shoes. The business donates 7,500 pairs of shoes to a charity that works to provide shoes to shoeless children living in underdeveloped nations. This charity gives each child one pair of shoes; the charity does this so all children can safely walk to and from their school. This means that the business and the charity value the quality of life, for one shoeless child living in an underdeveloped nation, at one pair of shoes.

Some of you reading those examples may think them callus. *They're not;* they are simply rational. The business that donated $9,000 (10% of its revenue) to charity was able to make that donation only because it had earned $90,000 in revenue, and its donation did not have a negative impact on its profit. Similarly, 7,500 pairs of shoes represented 5% of the shoe company's total expenses; the manufacturing of shoes costs money. The shoe company was able to manufacture 150,000 pairs of shoes, of which they then sold 142,500 pairs of shoes for a profit. Their profit allowed them to donate 7,500 pairs of their shoes to 7,500 shoeless children. The shoe company was also able to make this wonderful donation of 7,500 pairs of shoes without negatively impacting their profit.

So, what exactly is Quality of life? In humanatapilism, Quality of life is defined as the positive effect a humanatapilist business has on people when its donations do not have a negative impact on profit (revenue, total expenses or net profit). These positive effects on quality of life—the emotional, physical, and spiritual sense of well-being—are enjoyed by all in the humanatapilist transaction.

Attention new humanatapilist businesses: In a new humanatapilist business, changing even a small percentage of your donation, or changing even a small amount of what you donate can *massively change* your results. So, once a percentage or amount is established, you need to test its effects on profit. When you run your test, isolate one variable at a time. For example, If you choose to donate 10% of you revenue, you need to test to see what impact that donation will have on your profit (your revenue, total expenses, and net profit). Now, once you have an established quantity or percentage for your donation—

that is to say it does not negatively impact profit—you must continue making that donation for the rest of the foreseeable future. *Your donation is now a variable of your profit, and you are now a humanatapilist business.* As a humanatapilist business, your donations must be consistent—daily, weekly, monthly, quarterly, or yearly.

Note: If you choose to make an additional donation out of one of the other variables, you simply need to run a test to see what your donation's impact will be on that variable and the other variables.

Do not shoot yourself in the foot: Your business's first responsibility is to its profit. *Never* let your donations negatively impact your profit. *Profit first* allows humanatapilist businesses to evaluate the rational cost of Quality of life. Always remember what Abraham Lincoln said: "You can't help the poor by being one of them."

The Author, the Baker, and the News Anchor
Humanatapilism at Work

The Author—Aaron R. Lema

"Thank God they finally caught that crazy A-hole." That was my reaction after reading the newspaper headline that the serial killer has been captured. One of the murders had taken place just down the street from where I was living, and the other murders had all taken place within only a few miles. So to say I was happy this A-hole was caught would be an understatement. I just knew I was going to enjoy reading the rest of that article.

The article included a photo of a police officer talking to a bearded man sitting on the ground. The article went on to explain that the bearded man was homeless and that the officer was there to warn the homeless man of the dangers of being alone on the streets; the police believed the serial killer was preying on homeless men. Sadly, the article also went on to explain that the bearded man sitting in the photograph became the killer's fourth and last victim. The homeless man's name was John; he was a Vietnam War veteran and he had been savagely stabbed to death behind a fast food restaurant days after the photograph was taken. Witnesses to John's death led the police to the killer's whereabouts. John's death was the reason the killer was caught, and John's horrific death was the reason for the article. I was completely wrong—I truly hated reading that article.

I wish I could tell you that I made this story up, but it happened. John, 64, James, 53, Lloyd, 42 (only one year older than I am now), and Paulus, 57, were all brutally stabbed to death near where I live. Why? Who knows. The homeless, men, women, and children face many hardships and dangers while living on the streets; they go hungry, they sleep out in the elements, they get physically assaulted, and they even get murdered. Homelessness sucks.

I am donating 2.5% of my revenue, from the sale of this book, to Father Joe's village. Their programs provide sustenance, job training, heath care, and education for homeless people. And every single night more than 1,200 homeless people (men, women, children, and military vets) are safely sheltered by Father Joe's. Simply stated, homelessness sucks a lot less, and Father Joe's has the tools to improve the quality of life of homeless people. Father Joe's also has four other partner agencies that work to improve people's quality of life. One agency houses an additional 900 families, one provides long-term housing for homeless youth, one provides supportive housing for people suffering in isolation due to being HIV positive, and one serves over 250,000 meals annually to poor people. Father Joe's is able to accomplish all of this because they have a compassionate staff, dedicated volunteers, and generous donors. I encourage you to donate to Father Joe's Village.

Before you read on, I ask that you pray for John, James, Lloyd, Paulus, and their families. I also ask that you pray for the family of the A-hole; his actions caused them pain as well. I pray they find peace. As for the A-hole, I will leave that to God and our justice system.

The following short stories you are about to read are true. Only the names of the people and businesses portrayed have been changed. Okay, okay, they're totally fictional.

The Baker—Marvin

I enjoy bagels, give me a bagel with cream cheese, a slice of red onion, slice of tomato, and lox, and I'm really enjoying it. And Marvin, owner of Marvin's Bagels in L.A., makes the best bagels. But it's not their tasty bagels that I enjoy that got them into this book.

Marvin's Bagels donates 10% of its total expenses to charity, and that is what got them into this book—it's humanatapilist. Each day, the charity it supports picks up 25 of its bagels and delivers them to low-income, home-bound seniors—improving their quality of life. Those 25 bagels improving the seniors' quality of life represent 10% of Marvin's Bagels total expenses—making and baking of bagels cost money. So how does Marvin's Bagels donate 25 bagels a day to charity? Marvin bakes 250 bagels daily, sells 225 of those bagels to generate revenue, and sets aside the 25 bagels for charity. Since Marvin's Bagels generates more revenue than its total expenses, it earns a net profit. And Marvin's profitable operation of the business is what makes the donation of 25 bagels possible. That donation is one of the reasons I patronize Marvin's Bagels. The other reason? Their tasty bagels.

The News Anchor—William O'Malley

Mr. O'Malley is host of *The O'Malley Element*. His show is watched by millions of viewers, making it the most watched cable news program, and Mr. O'Malley is cable's most popular news anchor.

O'Malley's show provokes some and informs others with its just and equalized analysis of the day's pressing political and social issues. Using personal anecdotes along with a no-bull approach to interviewing a guest, O'Malley has endeared himself to his viewers. One thing is certain, whatever critics or fans label him, he is the big dog of cable news.

But that's not the reason O'Malley appears in this book.

Mr. O'Malley donates 10% of his net profit from his business, the cable news show, to charity. O'Malley is a humanatapilist—that, and my hope of some laudatory publicity, is why he appears in this book. The charity he supports, Village of Hope, is dedicated to improving the quality of life of orphaned and abandoned children. And this is how he does it. His news show generates revenue from the cable network it appears on. That revenue pays its total expenses. Because the show is successful, it earns more revenue than total expenses, which leaves his show with a net profit. Mr. O'Malley then donates 10% of the net profit to Village of Hope, and that donation improves the quality of life of orphaned and abandoned children. The fact that Mr. O'Malley is a humanatapilist is one reason I'm a fan of his show. I encourage you to donate to Village of Hope.

Attention: Humanatapilism is not only for authors, bakers, or news anchors—it's for any business generating more revenue than total expenses, thus earning a net profit.

People in a Humanatapilism Economy

Government's Role, How to Participate, How Not to Participate

Humanatapilism Is a Form of Free-Market Capitalism

Most of the people in a free-market capitalist society are baffled when it comes to the role of government in the economy. There is a very good reason it's called a free-market economy: Government must not *dictate* the direction the economy should take. When government is *allowed* to *dictate* the direction an economy should take, it stops being free. So what exactly is the government's role in a free market capitalist economy? Economist Milton Friedman's answer to that baffling question is this: "The existence of a free market does not of course eliminate the need for government. On the contrary, government is essential both as a forum for determining the rules of the game and as an umpire to interpret and enforce the rules decided on."

The rules decided on by the people of a free market capitalist society are simple. First, the primary mode of producing and distributing goods and services is privately owned and operated for private profit. Second, people are free to purchase or not purchase goods or services. Third, the government must provide the institutions, the forums, that work to protect the physical, intellectual, and contractual properties of its people and businesses, while providing a stable nonrestrictive, free-market, political climate in which to conduct business. Most importantly, *"We the people"*—not the government—are the economy.

Humanatapilism's main principle is the same principle that underlies the free-market capitalist system: *freedom*. In humanatapilism, as in free-market capitalism, no individual, organization, or political party can forcefully impose humanatapilism onto another individual, group, or business; participation in or cooperation with humanatapilism is *totally voluntary*.

One final thought on the government's role in the economy comes from James Madison, the fourth president of the United States. President Madison was also instrumental in drafting the first ten amendments to the U.S. constitution and was the key author of the U.S. Bill of Rights. *"Charity is in no part the legislative role of the government."*

How to Participate

In applying humanatapilism to real-life economic transactions, it is important to avoid *imposing* your value judgments or opinions onto others. Anyone not imposing value judgments or opinions onto others is called a humanatapilist; becoming a humanatapilist is how one participates in a humanatapilism economy. A humanatapilist is any person or business *willingly* and *honestly* participating in a humanatapilism economy.

Humanatapilism divides humanatapilists into three sectors: business owners, consumers, and public corporations. The first two, business owners and consumers, make up the largest sectors, while public corporations are the smallest sector. Public corporations have one additional variable in their humanatapilism formula, which will be explained later. For now, let's take a look at how each sector participates in a humanatapilism economy.

Sector one: Business owners. What is the role of business owners in free market capitalism? They act as the engines for economic expansion through the successful earning and distribution of their profits. Simply stated, successful business owner's activities propel the economy forward.

The role of business owners in humanatapilism is the same as that of business owners in free-market capitalism, with an additional quality-of-life benefit. I'll explain. A humanatapilist business's *quality of life* is improved by profit, profit is earned by supplying products or services to consumers that improve their *quality of life*, and finally, a set amount or a percentage of a humanatapilist business's profit is donated to charity to help improve the *quality of life* of our fellow human beings. Now that the additional quality-of-life benefit has been explained, let's show how business owners participate in humanatapilism.

Willingly and honestly is how business owners participate in humanatapilism. I'll start with *willingly*. All a business owner has to do is to decide to donate a percentage or set amount of their profit to charity—it's that easy.

Now, how to participate *honestly*? All business owners have to do to participate honestly is to make their donations known to the consumer. It's that easy—well, almost. Business owners who participate in humanatapilism should not impose their value judgments or opinions onto consumers. Example: I support Wounded Warrior Project, a charity working to improve the quality of life of our wounded veterans. I have an opinion on the wars we are engaged in, but I am not going to tell you what it is. And my opinions may be driven by my political beliefs, but I am not going to tell you what those are, either. My point is this: I support our veterans, and I do that by donating to Wounded Warrior Project. That is all I am going to tell you, the purchaser of my book, and that is all you should know. Okay, there's one more thing you should know: Wounded Warrior Project participates honestly in its charitable duties by helping all wounded veterans in need, regardless of their opinion on the war or their political beliefs. I encourage you to donate to Wounded Warrior Project.

What exactly is the role of business owners in humanatapilism? Simply stated, successful humanatapilist businesses propel the economy, and charitable donations, forward.

Sector two: The consumer. What is the role of the consumer in free-market capitalism? In free-market capitalism, individual consumers decide how best to use their resources—their money. Simply stated, consumers purchase goods or services that improve their quality of life.

The role of the consumer in a humanatapilism economy is exactly the same as the role of the consumer in free-market capitalism, with one additional quality-of-life benefit. Let me explain. When consumers buy from humanatapilist businesses, they get a product or a service that improves their *quality of life*, that humanatapilist business will make a profit improving its own *quality of life*, and finally, the humanatapilist business donates a percentage or a set amount of its profit to a charity to improve the *quality of life* of our fellow human beings. Wow, that mile-long sentence did explain the additional quality-of-life benefit, but it did not explain how consumers actively participate in humanatapilism. I'll do that now.

Willingly and honestly is how consumers actively participate in humanatapilism. Let us start with *willingly*. In a humanatapilism economy, a consumer will readily and cheerfully seek out a humanatapilist business to purchase from. Once again, *willing* is easy. *Honestly?* Now that's a different story.

When purchasing from a humanatapilist business, consumers should not impose their value judgments or opinions onto the humanatapilist business. Example: I support Father Joe's Village, a Catholic charitable organization, and you may not agree with the Catholic religion—heck, I'm a Catholic and I don't always agree. But I still support them, and that fact should not keep you from buying my book. Now, let me ask you this: I'm Caucasian; does this matter? If you answered no, than the fact that Father Joe's Village is a Catholic organization should not matter either. Note: Father Joe's Village participates honestly in its charitable actions, serving all people in need, regardless of their religious beliefs, skin color, or sexual orientation. One more note: If your answer was yes, my being a Caucasian does matter, and if that kept you from buying my book—then you suck.

So, what's the role of consumers in humanatapilism? Simply stated, consumers purchase goods or services that improve their own quality of life and, in a charitable way, the quality of life of our fellow human beings.

Attention: If the humanatapilist business gives poor service or sells shoddy products, do not buy from them, even if they do donate. Why waste money? Plus, there are plenty of businesses out there that want to give you good service or quality products—even if they do not donate. If all things are equal in terms of price, quality of service, or products, then you should choose humanatapilist businesses over non-humanatapilist businesses.

Sector three: Publicly traded corporations. *P squared = P (R – T = N) + S + D = Q* is the humanatapilism formula for publicly traded corporations. The S stands for Shareholder, and shareholders own shares of a publicly traded corporation's stock. The main duty of the publicly traded corporation is to make as much profit as possible, to increase shareholders' stock values. This duty may interfere with *D* or Donation; shareholders may not agree on donating, or they may not want to donate, choosing instead to reinvest profit back into the corporation. This duty is why publicly traded corporations are the smallest sector in humanatapilism.

The role of publicly traded corporations in humanatapilism is the same as that of the business owners. They also participate willingly and honestly as a humanatapilist business owner would. The only difference, and its slight, is in how to participate honestly. I'll explain.

How does a publicly traded corporation participate honestly in humanatapilism? They make *D* or Donation part of their corporate culture. An example: The publicly traded fast food restaurant McSomething has donated for decades to a charitable organization, we'll call it "The Thomas McSomething Home." This charitable organization provides housing for parents of sick children, so parents living far away from hospitals can be close to their children. McSomething is totally honest about its donations, placing corporate donation information and donation boxes in its restaurants—McSomething's has made Donation, or *D*, part of its corporate culture.

As a shareholder you have chosen to invest in a corporation. Your decision should take into account the corporation's corporate culture. In a humanatapilism economy, Donation, or *D*, is part of a corporation's corporate culture. Another benefit of charitable donations that shareholders should not overlook is the tax deductibility of *D* or donations.[2] This is a wash for shareholders—the amount donated to charity would have otherwise gone to pay the corporation's taxes.

So, what is the role of publicly traded corporations in humanatapilism? The successful publicly traded corporation's activities propel the economy forward, increase share values for shareholders, and enable charitable donations.

Before moving on:

While I was watching a program on businesses' donating, one person interviewed smugly stated, "We cannot buy our way to a cure."—that's totally false. My book won't cure autism, but I can donate a percentage of my profit from the sale of my book to Autism Speaks; that percentage of profit helps fund their research, and their research may lead to the cure—that's the truth.

How Not to Participate
(Caution: This section contains some salty language.)

In applying humanatapilism to real life economic transactions, it is important to avoid *imposing* your value judgments or opinions on others—wow, déjà vu, right. Anybody who imposes value judgments or personal opinions onto others is a JERK.[3] These JERKS are also humanatapilizing, and *humanatapilizing* is how *not* to participate. Humanatapilizing is defined as *profiting from humanatapilism in a fraudulent manner, or forcefully imposing humanatapilism onto a person or business through political actions or social pressures.*

Humanatapilism categorizes humanatapilizing scumbags[4] into two groups. The first group is *royal scumbags*; they are profiting from humanatapilism in a fraudulent manner. The second group is *arrogant scumbags*; they are forcefully imposing humanatapilism onto a person or business through political actions or social pressures. Royal scumbags are the worst, so I will save them 'til last; arrogant scumbags, on the other hand, are more prevalent, so I will start off with them.

Arrogant scumbags. Arrogant scumbags have an overbearing sense of self-importance, giving them a feeling of superiority over others. Unfortunately, arrogant scumbags are everywhere. They infest our political system, they're in our business communities, in our school systems, in our newsrooms, and even in our churches and community groups. Believe it or not, I even had to listen to two loud arrogant scumbags arguing with one another while I was waiting in a hospital emergency room. There is absolutely no way of avoiding them. You will have to deal with one or multiples of them at some point, so you must become familiar with their MOs, their modes of operation.

There are two basic modes of operation for the common arrogant scumbag, and I will explain each of them. The first mode of operation for the arrogant scumbag is to forcefully impose personal views onto a person or business through social pressures. The following are a few examples of this type of arrogant scumbag behavior.

---

2   Please consult a tax professional, because I am not one.
3   See JERK disclosure on MY GOAL page.
4   This is no joke; these people are actual scumbags.

"The thesaurus" arrogant scumbags. The thesaurus arrogant scumbag is the true master of twisting words to try and impose their views onto others. They know every synonym and every antonym of every word. They will tell you their anger is only passion and that your anger is animosity towards others. They tell you your charity is unkind while telling you their intolerant behavior is fair. Thesaurus arrogant scumbag's stink of the foul perfume that is insolence and their odor permeates through every scumbag category.

"Do as I say, not as I do" arrogant scumbags. They want others to donate because they say they cannot afford to donate. They also will join community organizations that try to force people and businesses to donate through social pressures. These community organizations use code names for their "Do as I say not as I do" activities—names like Social Fairness or Social Justice; these are simply names for extortion.

"I do not like that charitable organization; you must support one that I do like" arrogant scumbags. They are publicly pushy with their views and only want people or business to make donations to the charities *they* approve of. These arrogant scumbags protest outside of a person's home, a place of business, a charity's headquarters, or through the media outlets to try to force their views onto others.

"I will harass the charitable organization and make them stop taking donations from that person or business" arrogant scumbags. These people suck, they will totally try to stop charitable organizations from taking donations, just so they can impose their views onto others. I hope this type of scumbag finds a strange hair in their lunch.[5]

Most people, businesses, and charitable organizations can handle an arrogant scumbag's trying to forcefully impose personal views onto them through social pressures. They know an arrogant scumbag's bluster will soon blow over, and any wounds they may have caused will heal quickly.

The second mode of operation takes a little thicker skin to deal with. The second mode of operation for the arrogant scumbag is to forcefully impose personal views onto a person or business through political actions. These arrogant scumbags are using *bogus political actions* to try to force their views onto others. The following are examples of this type of arrogant scumbag's behavior.

"I'll sic my representative on you" arrogant scumbags. Theses arrogant scumbags have the attention, or scorn, of their local or national political representatives and they are not afraid to use it, or exploit it, to get their views imposed onto other people. These types of arrogant scumbags work hand in hand with the next type of arrogant scumbag.

Pandering-politician arrogant scumbags. Pandering-politician arrogant scumbags are, or may be former, "I'll sick my representative on you" arrogant scumbags. They will use their political offices and their political influences to forcefully impose their views onto others. Pandering-politician arrogant scumbags will do this out of a fear of losing voters, or they will do it as a way of attracting new voters. Pandering-politician arrogant scumbags suck. I not only hope they find a strange hair in their lunch; I also hope they spill their drink in their lap.

---

[5]   I'm not advocating placing strange hairs in people's lunches.

Now that I have given you some examples of arrogant scumbag behavior, I feel it's my responsibility to explain some possible ways of avoiding run-ins with arrogant scumbags. Look, arrogant scumbags are wily characters; they will attack you at any level, *no matter how low*, and this makes it very difficult for good people and honest businesses to defend against them. However, it's not hard to slip under their radar. There are two strategies to slipping under the arrogant scumbag's radar, and I will tell you both.

The simplest strategy is, "Never argue with stupid people, they will drag you down to their level and beat you with experience." Those words of wisdom were written over a hundred years ago by Mark Twain, and they still hold true today.

The second way is not politically correct—but it happens to be the most effective: Stay far away from reproductive, sexual-orientation, and political charities if you want to avoid run-ins with arrogant scumbags. The arrogant scumbags on *either side* of these hot-button issues will hurl their self-righteous hatred onto you like a troop of pissed-off, dung-flinging chimps, and then they'll go to work on you. You don't have to believe me; just watch all the self-righteous dung flung my way for having given this warning. God help me.[6]

Note: You're *totally free* to support any charitable organization, including, a reproductive, sexual orientation, or political charity—just don't come crying to me if a cantankerous arrogant scumbag takes to flinging dung at you.

Royal scumbags. They're hemorrhoids; when they appear, they're pains in the butt. Royal scumbags are liars, cheats, low lifes, and frauds. Royal scumbags have elastic ethics and malleable morals—even the arrogant scumbags say these people are no good. Unfortunately, royal scumbags exist; the newspapers, television news shows, and watch-dog organizations expose royal scumbags on a regular basis. There is absolutely no way to stop them; their total disregard for ethical behavior ensures they will always be among us, and that's the truth.[7] Royal scumbags have three basic narcissistic modes of operation; I will give you one simple example for each.

> ***"We donate to protect our phony baloney jobs" royal scumbags.*** These royal scumbags use their donations to try and polish their tarnished image. An example of this scumbag's behavior: The producers of small paper-wrapped roles of finally cut tobacco for smoking,[8] making donations to charitable organizations to help fight lung cancer. Their donation is made to try and improve their public image, or, their donation is made to try and appease their pissed-off or sickened customers. These types of donations *are not* humanatapilism donations—*the royal scumbag's product or service, caused the problem.*

> ***"We must cover our butts with a donation" royal scumbags.*** These royal scumbags use their donations as damage-control tools. An example of this type of behavior: A business *knowingly violates* environmental laws; when the business is caught by the authorities and starts catching heat from the public for its environmental crime, the business begins to donate to environmental groups to try to appease the public and activist groups. These types of donations *are not* humanatapilism donations—*the royal scumbags unscrupulous actions caused the problem.*

---

6   Sadly, in this day and age, that statement is not politically correct, either.
7   These are my honest opinions. If you don't like them, tough.
8   Their product has been linked by the U.S. Surgeon General to lung cancer and other serious health risks.

Some people, politicians, and activist groups may see these types of donations as a means of righting wrongs; humanatapilists see these types of donations as hypocritical. I loathe these royal scumbags, but they're *totally free* to make those types of donations. They cannot, however, make those donations in the name of humanatapilism.

Klepto-Madeoff-Illgottenitus royal scumbags. These types of royal scumbags have an obsessive impulse to steal from others—*even from charitable organizations*. These royal scumbags collect monies for charitable organizations and then keep the monies for themselves. Klepto-Madeoff-Illgottenitus royal scumbags are the very worst type of scumbag. They not only need to find a strange hair in their lunch and spill their drink in their lap, they need to do it while sitting in a jail cell.

Now that I have explained Klepto-Madeoff-Illgottenitus, I feel it is my responsibility to tell you that there is absolutely no way to stop it. People like this have been with us since the dawn of civilization, and they will be with us 'til the end of civilization. However, we can *levy fines* on them[9] or put them in jail. Let me explain how.

If you're aware, or become aware, of a Klepto-Madeoff-Illgottenitus royal scumbag's actions, you must inform the police or the IRS.[10] The Klepto-Madeoff-Illgottenitus royal scumbag collected money for a charitable organization and then kept it—this is fraud. If they were dumb enough to claim the money they have taken on their taxes as a charitable tax deduction—this is tax fraud. They should *be fined* or jailed for these scumbag actions.

Warning: Pandering-politician arrogant scumbags may use the IRS as a tool to impose their views.[11] We need the *honest people* at the IRS to blow the whistle or leak info on this type of scumbag behavior—*even if you voted for those politicians*.

---

9   The only thing these scumbags value is money.
10   Yes, I want you to nark them off—they're scumbags. Warning: Do not make a false claim, or it could be your butt fined and in jail.
11   Yes, I do think pandering politicians, or their political cronies, would stoop to this. God help me again.

Charitable Organizations

The Catalyst of the Humanatapilism Economy

Charity, preached by every major religion, is a way to spread humanity throughout one's community. And charity is the bedrock of humanatapilism. Humanatapilism has therefore made charity obligatory[12] and binding[13] to all seeking to participate in it; *D*, or Donation, was embedded into humanatapilism to give charity consistency and permanence. However, having consistency and permanence is useless if *D*, or Donation, does not have a direction. That's where charitable organizations come in—*they provide that direction.*

The Purpose of Charitable Organizations

Charitable organizations, the catalyst of the humanatapilism economy, work to give our *D*, or Donation, a sense of direction in the humanatapilism economy—*a purpose, if you will*. Charities provide valuable services for people in need; services such as delivering meals to low-income seniors, helping our wounded veterans recover from physical or emotional wounds, and providing sustenance for homeless people. Simply stated, *charities improve people's quality of life*. It's their ability to facilitate charitable transactions, the collecting and distributing of our *D*, or Donations, that bonds charities to businesses and people in a humanatapilism economy. This bond is humanatapilism's strength.

Choosing a Charitable Organization

Choose a charity you're passionate about, or a charity that performs a service you value. This will give you the greatest quality of life. Are you concerned with poverty, homelessness, or our veterans' health? Or would you like to help impoverished children living in an underdeveloped nation? Are you going to donate money, products, services, or expertise? Theses are questions you will need to answer; choose wisely.

Look Before You Leap

Charitable organizations are always in need of our donations. It's a good idea to do some research on the charitable organization before you donate. I believe everyone reading this book values the contributions charitable organizations have made to our society, and I want that to endure. This will only happen if donors are sure the charity is utilizing the D, or Donation, wisely. Some nonprofit organizations evaluate or rate charitable organizations. These organizations give donors valuable insight into charities; insight that can help donors make educated *D*, or Donation, decisions. The two major ones are *Charity Navigator[14] and *Charity Watch.[15,16] *Note:* small and locally based charities may not be rated or evaluated by these organizations; in those cases, you must do your own research.

---

12   Profit must be earned successfully, and donations must be made willingly and honestly.
13   Donation is a variable of profit.
14   Charity Navigator is a charity rating/evaluating site and is a 501(c)3 nonprofit charitable organization. Its website is www.charitynavigator.org. Charity Navigator has *in no way* endorsed this book or its contents.
15   American Institute of Philanthropy dba Charity Watch is a charity rating/evaluating site; it is a 501(c)3 nonprofit organization. Its website is www.charitywatch.org. American Institute of Philanthropy dba Charity Watch has in no way endorsed this book or its contents.
16   The above-mentioned organizations are in no way responsible for this book or its contents. *I am*

Don't Even Think About It!

When to Exclude Businesses from Humanatapilism

Humanatapilism is not social justice, collective salvation, a social responsibility of business, progressivism, or American progressivism. *Instead, it is a form of free-market capitalism.*

Temporarily Excluded from Humanatapilism

Any business, public or private, that receives a government bailout or government subsidies is excluded from participating in a humanatapilism economy. There are three reasons for making these exclusions:

1. A bailed out business was unable to profitably participate in a free-market capitalist economy; without government intervention, it would have failed.
2. A subsidized business is incapable of participating profitably in a free-market capitalist economy; without governmental assistance, it would earn losses and fail.
3. A donation provided by a bailed-out or subsidized business would be a donation made at taxpayers' expense; the business earned no profit and therefore cannot be allowed to donate.

The exclusion shall remain in effect until the following conditions are met:

- The bailed out business must pay back all monies to the government and then post ten consecutive years of *real profitability*.
- The subsidized business must stop taking any government assistance and then post ten consecutive years of *real profitability*.

Note: Tax breaks for public or private companies are not subsidies; tax breaks are when the government *takes less* of what a business *rightfully* and *successfully earns*.

Permanently Excluded from Humanatapilism

Any business that *subsidizes* its labor force by using illegal workers is permanently excluded. There are two good reasons for not allowing these businesses to participate.

1. A business *subsidizing* its workforce cannot participate profitably in a free-market capitalist economy; without *exploiting* people, the business would earn losses.
2. We cannot import misery in the name of exporting a higher quality of life; we also can not attain a higher quality of life by illegally exploiting others.

Finally, for-profit prisons and jails are excluded for two good reasons:

1. Any society that passes laws and establishes penalties for breaking those laws must bear the cost of incarcerating those that are being punished.
2. Any donation made by for-profit prisons or jails would be at an incarcerated person's expense; and that, I believe, would be immoral.

---

not affiliated with either organization.

Final Thoughts

Which of the charitable models do you believe is more likely to pay greater attention to the desires of its contributors by utilizing the most efficient and most effective methods of distributing the resources (dollars, products, services, or expertise) contributed to it? Is it a non-profit charitable organization whose directors are accountable to its contributors who seek out the most bang, *Quality of life*, for their donations? Or is it a government-run welfare (charity) program seen as a line item in some budget by politicians, to be bickered over for their own political purposes without any regard for the people who contribute to it *through taxation*? If you answered the former, I welcome you to humanatapilism. If you answered government-run welfare, you're wrong, and you totally wasted your time and money when you chose to purchase this book. *Sorry, no refunds.*

> "If you explain something so clearly that no one can misunderstand it, someone will."
> —Murphy's Law

For some people in economic conversations about free-market capitalism it becomes more important for them to be right, or for them to *feel right*, than it is for them to listen to the other person. These types of people spend most of their time in the conversation thinking about their rebuttal to what the other person is saying instead of truly listening to the other person; this is because they have *predetermined* that person to be wrong. When this B.S. happens in conversations, the conversations rapidly turn into an argument. Instead of listening and seeking to comprehend the other person's values, these people become even more determined to impose their values onto the other person. Sometimes this will lead to name calling or vicious personal attacks, in the hopes of imposing their values. When it reaches the idiotic level of name calling and personal attacks, nothing gets accomplished.

> "If you try to please everyone, someone is not going to like it."
> —Murphy's Law

The bottom line is this: Humanity is subjective and it makes value judgments, while free-market capitalism is objective and cannot make value judgments. It is within the realm of value judgments that free-market capitalism is *getting screwed*. The reality is that free-market capitalism has a humanity problem, not the other way around. If you choose to agree with me on this, then welcome again to humanatapilism. If you choose to disagree with me, then I truly couldn't care less. Either way, I thank you for purchasing my book.

> "We have it in our power to begin the world over again."
> —Thomas Pain

It is my belief that any economic model that is to play a significant role in the quality of life of people in any society must be free market, and include an emotional/rational approach. Ultimately, *We the people,* not the government, will determine how and when that economic model will be implemented—so let's get off our butts and do this thing.

$1,000,000 for Charity

$250,000 for Four Charities

My goal for this book is to raise $250,000 for each of four outstanding charitable organizations: $250,000 for Autism Speaks, $250,000 for Father Joe's Village, $250,000 for Wounded Warrior Project, and $250,000 for Village of Hope.

The above-mentioned charitable organizations do great works that *improve people's quality of life*, and that is why 10% of my revenue from the sale of my book will be donated to them.

Fine Print Disclosures

Autism Speaks has in no way endorsed this book or its contents. Father Joe's Village has in no way endorsed this book or its contents. Wounded Warrior Project has in no way endorsed this book or its contents. Village of Hope (Kingdom Adventures) has in no way endorsed this book or its contents.

The above mentioned charitable organizations are in *no way* responsible for this book or its contents.

DON'T BE A JERK. If you do not like this book or its contents *do not blame or harass* the above mentioned charities; they had absolutely nothing to do with it. (Nothing, nada, zero, zip, and zilch I tell you!) And their appearance in this book does not mean they did; it only means I want to give the above mentioned charities $250K, and that $250K will be used to *improve people's quality of life*, so please—DON'T BE A JERK.

> JERK Disclosure: *JERK* is the sole opinion of the author, and *it does not* reflect the opinion of any of the above mentioned charitable organizations.
>
>> JERK Disclosure Disclosure: *JERK* is for entertainment purposes only; it should not be taken seriously by anyone. This includes JERKS, the BIG JERKS that may represent them, and any REPRESENTATIVE JERKS in government.

MORE ABOUT THE ABOVE-MENTIONED CHARITABLE ORGANIZATIONS: If you would like more information about the above-mentioned charitable organizations or if you would like to make a charitable donation to one of them, please visit their organization websites: www.autismspeaks.org, my.neighbor.org, www.supportwwp.org, and www.kingdomadventures.org, respectively. All these web addresses are current as of this printing.

SIDE EFFECT OF CHARITABLE DONATION: A heightened sense of emotional, physical, and spiritual wellbeing. "Any person who contributes to prosperity must prosper in return." —Earl Nightingale

ALLOCATION OF PROCEEDS FROM SALE OF THIS BOOK. Ten percent (10%) of my royalties and/or revenue (as the case may be) from sale of this book will be donated to charity. The 10% will be divided equally, with 2.5% going to each of the four above-mentioned charitable organizations. Payments to charitable organizations will be made as royalty checks are received, or payments to charitable organizations will be made every quarter of a calendar year—the first payment being made on April 1, the second payment on July 1, the third payment on Oct 1, and the final payment on Dec 31. Note: Donations of 2.5% of royalties, or revenue from this book, per charitable organization will continue to be made after the $1,000,000 goal has been achieved: *As long as this book continues to sell, I will continue to donate.*

ATTENTION: I reserve all rights to the donations: This includes the ability to cease donations at my discretion at any time and without any notice, the ability to apply the donations to other charitable organizations, the ability to combine donations into larger donations, and the ability to change the percentage donated. *Any and all changes made to the donations will be noted in future printings.* This particular disclosure sucks—but it had to be stated.

www.ingramcontent.com/pod-product-compliance
Lightning Source LLC
Chambersburg PA
CBHW081821170526
45167CB00008B/3488